Rodney B. James

Finding

Your

Virtue

Realize Your Value.   Get Better Not Bitter.
Become the Pursued.

Copyright © 2012 by Rodney B. James

ISBN-10: 1937705137
ISBN-13: 978-1-19377051-3-8
Also available in E-book:
ISBN-13: 978-1-19377050-1-5
Library of Congress Control Number: 2011938752
Printed in the United States of America

M

MavLit Publishing, LLC
www.maverick-books.com
P. O. Box 1103
Irmo, S.C. 29063

Cover Design: Maverick Literary
Cover Photos: Getty Images

CONTENTS

Rodney B. James

Finding

Your

Virtue

Realize Your Value.   Get Better Not Bitter.
Become the Pursued.

INTRODUCTION

In the Bible, there is a familiar passage of scripture (Proverbs 31:1-31) that deals with the virtuous woman. This text will serve as foundational scripture; and throughout this book, I will be referring to it in the context of a woman's goal to becoming a virtuous woman.

This book is targeted for the contemporary woman of this society that we live in today; however, know that God's word is timeless. Various lifestyles have become the norm—not just the norm for those in the world today—but they have also become the norm for people in the house of God.

As a pastor, I have an opportunity to observe these lifestyles, and there are times when a pastor who has oversight of a church must address these lifestyles that are lived by his or her congregation.

It's the biblical mandate to every preacher of the Word of God to proclaim and declare God's Word, His precepts, principles, and standards to every generation. Though every generation is different, God's standards remain the same. Much of what has become socially acceptable in our society is contrary to God's Word, and it is the job of the preacher to declare to us that we've crossed the line of God's law. It's what Elijah did with Ahab and Jezebel; it's what Jonah was sent to Nineveh to do; it's what John the Baptist did in the wilderness; and it's still our job today as those who are entrusted with the care of His people.

We also see a plethora of biblical inconsistencies in the make up of our contemporary church: There is no shortage of dead-beat dads, Pentecostal pimps, tyrannical teens, curt kids, unwed mothers, and unfit moms. Not to mention, the church is soiled by extramarital affairs, openly gay males and females, and long-term living together arrangements.

Being a pastor of a local church, I am often spiritually grieved by what I've seen in the lifestyle of the people I've been privileged to pastor. But out of all the people who comprise the local church, one group of people stand out above all others: the women of the local church.

Now, I have to admit that this group is not hard to notice since it is the largest group making up fifty to sixty-five percent—or more—of many congregations. Shockingly, very few people have recognized the impact of a woman's lifestyle on her family, community, and the world because a woman's lifestyle is crucial to having healthy families, morally correct communities, and in the development of moral societies worldwide.

Traditionally, we're taught that men are the most important factor in developing healthy families, communities, and societ-ies. While that is true in many regards, because biblically men have been given headship and have be elevated to a position of responsibility *for* the family, community, and society, men by no means wield the kind of influence that women wield *over* the fam-ily, community and society, through a connection with their chil-dren—just ask Jacob about it Gen. 27: 1-30.

The reason why the woman is so important in all of this is be cause she is not only a woman, she's also a mother. Now, I know some women have never had children due to medical reasons, or simply by choice. And that's fine. But whether a woman admits to it or not, every woman in some way is mothering somebody. Sometimes she's doing it without actually knowing it.

Because of this, a woman holds the most influential position known to man, and that is the position of a mother. Mothers are influential in the lives of their children because most of the morals that a child ever learns comes from his or her mother; a mother is often a child's first teacher because many things are imparted into a child by his or her mother that, in many ways, are hard to reverse.

That kind of influence can be a major factor in determining what kind of man her son becomes or what kind of woman her daughter becomes. Therefore, the maternal factor is imperative to her family and community. But the maternal factor is not the only reason why the lifestyle lived by a woman is so important; it is much more involved than that. Everything from finances to ca reers are connected to the kind of lifestyle a woman leads—even her success in relationships has to do with her lifestyle.

This book will use the biblical principles taught to us by the virtuous woman of Proverbs 31 to guide and lead women to a rich, full, and virtuous life.

CHAPTER 1

Wise Advice to Men of Wisdom

What is very clear in Proverbs 31 is the way King Lemuel's mother frames her advice to him. She warns him that the lifestyle he leads should be befitting of a king, and it should not include a woman who would lead him to his ruin. Then she goes into great detail about the kind of woman who would better complement him and is a reflection of excellence in his life, and ultimately gives God the glory.

Note her opening remarks:

> (1).The words of King Lemuel, the prophecy that his mother taught him. (2). What my son? And what the son of my womb? And what, the son of my vows. (3). Give not thy strength unto women, nor thy ways to that which destroyeth kings. (King James Version, Prov. 31: 1-3)

When reading the first three verses in the King James Version there is not much light shed on the depth of the wisdom in this passage. Even the Living Bible doesn't really do justice to this text, although the third verse does mention that a young king should not waste his youth and life potential on the kind of woman who might ruin him. But the same verses from the Message Bible offer greater insight.

Note what is said:

> (1). The words of king Lemuel, the strong advice his mother gave him: (2). Oh son of mine, what can you be thinking of Child whom I bore. The son I dedicated to God. Don't dissipate your virility on fortune-hunting women, promiscuous women who shipwreck leaders. (Message Bible Translation, Prov. 31:1-3)

This translation reveals that King Lemuel's mother has advised her son of the kind of women whom he should avoid. In other words, she begins her dialogue with her son by instructing him on what a virtuous woman is not. This eliminates any chance of confusion, and she has effectively minimized the chance of her son being deceived by a woman who is not virtuous, but is pretending to be so.

It is possible for a woman to look virtuous and not be virtuous at the same time? Yes. That's because looks can be deceiving. In some cases, all that is required for a virtuous appearance is the right outfit or dress. But you do know that virtuous clothing is also sold to women who aren't virtuous, so then virtue is more than a look.

You can also talk and profess virtue with your mouth and still not possess any because talk is cheap. Virtue is not just what you say or what you wear. It is who you are and what you do. The Bible exhorts us to add to our faith, virtue. There's a reason for that. Virtue is more than a profession. It's more than a look. It's a lifestyle. Now, whether we admit it or not, our lifestyle deter-mines who and what we are, and you can not live one lifestyle and profess to live another lifestyle.

Now, notice the lifestyle of the women she warns her son against. There is nothing about that type of lifestyle that is virtu-ous. Let's look at these:

'REFUSE TO BE USED'

King Lemuel's mother warns her son about the type of woman who is in it for what she can get out of it. This is a woman who wants something from a man before she gets to know the man.

A gold digger does whatever it takes to get the material things that she wants from a man whether he is her husband or not. She is akin to a prostitute because if sex gets her what she wants, she'll do it without hesitation. For this kind of woman, love and virtue are not priorities; money and compensation are. The dan-ger in getting involved with this kind of woman is her motivation, and she's motivated by greed and not love.

Therefore, with greed as the motivating factor in her life, her loyalty is for sale to the highest bidder. She is more loyal to money than she could ever be to the one whom she is supposed to love.

'AVOIDING TIES'

The second type of woman King Lemuel's mother warns him not get involved with is a loose or promiscuous woman. She warns that this kind of woman can literally destroy a king just by her lifestyle alone.

Unlike the gold digger, this type of woman is incapable of being committed to anything or anyone. She is also a woman who has not established self-worth or value in her life. Although some of you may disagree with me about this, but in a few ways the gold digger is better off. At least she is safer to deal with than the loose or promiscuous woman. The gold digger is at least committed to something, even if it is money. And she has in some way established self-worth. But the loose or promiscuous is not committed to anything or any one, nor has she established any value or self-worth.

You see, she can't be committed to anyone because she keeps creating what I like to call "gluing experiences." I use the term gluing experiences in reference to sex. Now, in relationships (marriage) sex is very much like glue because it solidifies the relationship. That's why when a couple gets married from the Bible days to the present if they don't consummate it (have sex) then the marriage is not valid.

The consummating of the marriage solidifies the marriage vows made to each other under God. Every time you have sex (i.e., a gluing experience) you literally join yourself to the other person.

Now, this joining is not just at the physical level but much deeper. Sex is spiritual because you're gluing yourself to whatever that person is, or whatever spirits that are in them. It's what someone else has referred to as a "Soul Tie," a joining of spirits. But, remember, there are good and bad spirits out there. Therefore, you literally tie yourself to that person—and one of those spirits control or influence that person—which also may influence or control you.

Although it may have been easy to tie yourself, it is most often very difficult to untie yourself. The reason for the difficulty in untying yourself is that you have applied the glue (sex) to this relationship. That is why some women stay in unhealthy, ungodly, and abusive relationships. It's not because they don't want out; they can't untie themselves.

Biologically speaking, women produce more of the hormone oxytocin, which is known as the bonding hormone for them. For men, this hormone is secreted after sex; it is when they are more apt to "bond" or feel closer to a woman. That's why you should never engage in premarital sex because you maybe tying yourself to something that you want to untie later.

Ever wonder why some women won't leave men who won't marry them, miss treat them, and even physically abuse them? It's because they can't. This syndrome becomes so muddled to the point of them being dumped and abandon by these men. The woman then gets involved in another relationship, but she will continue to have sex with the man who abandoned her. That's why some women can't glue to the one they've said "I do" because they have all these other gluing experiences to compare it to.

Therefore, the loose or promiscuous woman is unstable at best because she is tied in so many places that she can't possibly be faithful to just one man.

'A Mother's Warning to Her Son'

King Lemuel's mother also told him that these kinds of women ruin kings. They ruin kings by getting them off focus. He becomes engrossed by keeping the unfaithful woman faithful and in line, or trying to lavish the gold digger with expensive gifts so that he might not be outdone and out-pimped by another king, which may lead to the affairs of the kingdom lacking. He begins to make unwise decisions because he can't concentrate on what really matters.

Some of you might say that if the kingdom crumbles it's not the gold digger or the loose woman's fault since he is the king. While it is true that he is the king, he is also the same person who was king when the kingdom prospered. It was only when he hooked up with those kinds of women when the kingdom crumbled. And why was that? It's because she did not add peace and joy to his heart.

Rather, she brought stress and frustration; or in other words, he became discombobulated.

Say what you will, but when you're out of whack everything you do is out of whack. In fact when you couple the first three verses with verse 4, it almost appears that Lemuel's mother is saying to him that these kinds of women can drive a good man to drinking.

Let me say this to the women who are waiting on their king to come along. Whenever a king gets ready to marry, he bears in mind that if he wants to remain as the king he cannot marry just anybody.

So, therefore, he is very selective about who he dates and whom he's even seen with. Here's why: If she does not check out or measure up, to remain with her he has to abdicate the throne and he can never be king again.

Even the prince who wants to be king some day knows this. So the bride has to be checked out long before he starts wooing her. And what does he check? Her pedigree to see if she is of royal blood and her background; therefore, women of virtue always checkout because they're daughters of the kingdom and their father is the King of Kings and Lord of Lords.

How do you know that they are daughters of the kingdom? They live by the word of God.

CHAPTER 2

A Woman to Be Admired

I invited a friend of mine, Reverend Kimberly Moore, to preach the message to the women of our church for the Annual Women's Day Worship. I will never forget that message. It was a powerful word for the women. Her message was nothing deep or profound. And if it was, its profundity was stunningly simplistic. In fact, it was nothing that I had not heard before, but for some reason it captivated me. I had listened to the message rather than just hearing the words.

In her sermon, she declared a simple truth to the women: "God is raising our standards. He's raising the bar for women of God, and there is a standard God wants us to live by."

As I heard that, it resonated with me in a way that had never occurred before. I was compelled to agree with Rev. Moore's message and after much praying and searching, I realized why. I came to understand that God wanted me to talk with the daughters of the house about being godly women, and not just in name or appearance.

There is a standard that God wants the women and the men of God to live by. And the passage in Proverbs 31 deals with the standard that God has for a virtuous woman. He wants you to know that every woman possesses virtue. She merely has to tap into it. So let's meet this virtuous woman and unlock the virtuous woman within you.

Here is what must be undoubtedly the most read passage of scripture pertaining to women and their character, the "virtuous woman" of Proverbs 31:

> "Who can find a virtuous woman? For her price is far above rubies. The heart of her husband does safely trust in her, so that he shall have no need of spoil. She will do him good and not evil all the days of her life." (KJV, Prov.31: 10 – 12)

There are many women in this contemporary society who are to be admired. But if you're going to admire any virtue in these women, as this book and the Bible proclaims as a woman's most admirable quality, it might be helpful to know what to look for.

One of the characteristics of a virtuous woman is that she is admired. That is, as other women observe the attributes and characteristics that this woman exudes and possesses, they desire to be like her.

Now, there are women you know who are out there doing their thing, so to speak, and they are in the public eye for the entire world to see. However, very few of them could be considered virtuous. That's not to say that they aren't kind, caring, and compassionate people, but it's just that the kind of lifestyle they lead by biblical standards is far from virtuous.

Hollywood has more than its share of women who live together with men to whom they are not married. Not to mention, there are many who are having children born out of wedlock in these long-term living together arrangements. Then there are women out there who appear to have almost no virtues, and that list seems to get longer with each passing year. Lil Kim, Courtney Love, and Trina are just a few examples of these kinds of women, who coincidently are being watched by your children. But virtuous women are not admired because of star power, fashion sense, or wealth, but because she's godly.

So what makes her virtuous, you might ask?

'A VIRTUOUS APPEARANCE'

Well, first of all, she's virtuous in appearance. She doesn't wear just anything, but what she wears flatters her. You will never find a virtuous woman in any apparel that could be considered degrading nor will you see her in anything skimpy. She realizes that what she wears says a lot about the kind of woman she is. Therefore, she is godly in her appearance.

Verse 22 in Proverbs 31 tells us how this virtuous woman is dressed. The King James Version says:

> "She maketh herself coverings of tapestry; her clothing is silk and purple." (KJV, Prov. 31:22)

Now when you read this verse in the King James, it really doesn't do it justice. But when you read it in the Living Bible Translation, I believe that it adds much needed light. Note its translation of the same verse:

> "She quilts here own bedspreads. She dresses like royalty in gowns of finest cloth." (Living Bible Translation, Prov. 31:22).

This verse is packed with revelation about how much thought, time, and detail the woman who desires to be virtuous should put into what she wears. Notice the text says she dresses like royalty. Have you ever been in the presence of royalty? Well, if you have, then you know that when royalty is in a room no one has to point out whom that individual is. You just kind of know. Now a lot of that has to do with the way he or she dresses.

Can you even imagine the Queen of England dressing in any other way other than the way she already does? Probably not. And if you could, it would probably make you laugh to think about her any other way. Well now, don't feel bad if you couldn't, because she probably can't see herself any other way, either.

Why?

Because what she wears says she is the queen long before she says a word. Now, before you go out on a shopping spree and buy clothes you can't afford, trying to achieve virtue by looking like royalty, remember that the queen has something that not everyone has: money and lots of it.

I think it goes without saying that a woman can achieve a virtuous look without going into debt or trying to become the local fashion plate. After all, it is implied that this woman of the text made her own clothing; she just used good materials in the process. Designer labels like Prada, Fendi, DKNY, and Burberry are nice, but many women have achieved virtue without them.

'A VIRTUOUS CONVERSATION'

Secondly, this woman is virtuous in her conversation. That's right, even your conversation is an indication of virtue. A virtuous woman doesn't let just anything flow from her lips, but she carefully weighs every word to ensure that they are helpful and not harmful.

Listen to what King Lemuel's mother says about a virtuous woman's conversation as she tells him what to look for in a woman/wife:

> "She openeth her mouth with wisdom: and in her tongue is the law of kindness." (KJV, Prov. 31:26)

King Lemuel's mother makes it crystal clear to her son and to us today that the conversation of a virtuous woman should be filled with wisdom. I believe that if we are really honest with ourselves we would have to admit that a significant amount of what we like to talk about is unwise at best. I know this because although I'm a man, men and women's conversations differ very little in substance. Men often criticize women for having a gossiping spirit and for having an appetite for the latest news. But the real truth of the matter is that the conversations held in the beauty salons aren't much different from the ones in the barber shop—at least as far as substance is concerned.

Now that subject right there is enough to write a book. But if a woman is to be virtuous, she must not engage in conversations that are harmful and malicious in nature. That's right. A virtuous woman is wise enough to know that she should never talk about a person, but she talks to the person. After all, she knows that talking about someone or something does not in anyway help solve the problem but it adds to it.

King Lemuel's mother didn't waste time and energy in Proverbs 31 talking to someone else about her son, but she talked directly to him. The King James Version of the Bible almost suggests that she didn't open her mouth unless she had something wise to say. The Message Bible translation says that when she spoke she always had something worthwhile to say.

There's another thing that becomes clear in that passage as you read the same verse in the Living Bible Translation:

> "When she speaks, her words are wise, and kindness is the rule when she gives instruction." (LBT, Prov 31:26)

The "B" clause of this verse tells us that her conversation is instructional in nature, and her instructions are kind. The text suggests that the woman of Proverbs 31 is a wise woman who offers advice but not just any advice; it is both sound and inviting.

Notice the virtue King Lemuel's mother displays as she lovingly instructs and counsels her son. She doesn't degrade him or engage in an argument with him, but she gently guides him down the right path.

'Virtuous Lifestyle'

Finally, this woman is regarded as virtuous by her lifestyle. One of the most poignant verses in Proverbs 31 deals with the lifestyle of the virtuous woman. This is found in the 11th verse.

> "The heart of her husband doth safely trust in her, so that he shall have no need of spoil." (KJV, Prov. 31:11)

If you pay close attention to the verse, it points out something that is very significant about the virtuous woman's lifestyle. It makes clear that virtuous women are not interested in ungodly relationships. The verse clearly says to us that the heart of her husband safely trusts in her. The text says nothing about her boyfriend, her man, lover, or same-sex partner.

No, this woman has a husband and he's not someone else's. The virtuous woman of Proverbs 31 upholds, believes in, and demonstrates the biblical example of family. She understands that since the beginning of time God has had a design for the family, and the components of it are a man and a woman who are also a husband and a wife to each other.

As you examine the biblical context of relationships between men and women you'll find that there's not a whole lot in there about girlfriends and boyfriends, same-sex coupling, or even long-term cohabitation arrangements. But it for the most part deals with the relationship between a man and a woman as husbands and wives.

The virtuous woman doesn't waste her time in relationships that are not headed toward that eventuality. I think I also need to point out that the virtuous woman knows how to conduct herself in a relationship with a man to ensure that she has the right man, and that man is going to do the right thing by her. But we'll talk more about this in the chapters to come.

CHAPTER 3

A Woman of Value

T he virtuous woman should be a woman of value and not just to herself but to her husband, her children, and to her community.

In verse 10 it reads:

> Who can find a virtuous woman? For her price is far above rubies. (KJV, Prov. 31:10)

The "A" clause of this verse suggests that this is no ordinary woman who can be found any and everywhere, but that she is a rare find who has to be sought out.

As you know, the rarer something is the more valuable it is. Take gold and diamonds, for instance. The reason they are more valuable than aluminum and crystal is because they aren't as plentiful.

The same can be said about virtuous women. They are not in great supply, and are therefore hard to find. Now this is not to say that there is a shortage of women. No, quite the contrary, the world is filled with women of all types. But I think what Lemuel's mother is suggesting is that so few of them have tapped into the virtue within themselves.

I told you at the outset of this book that every woman possesses virtue. Thereby, she has the potential to become virtuous. However, that virtue has to be nurtured and matured.

Now, I need to pause here long enough to say that there are several contributing factors as to why the virtue within some women may never be nurtured and become mature. Those factors can be anything from society's value system, environment, lack of good role models, and even poor parenting. But the main focus of this chapter is to assert when a woman matures in virtue, she becomes even more valuable. In fact, she is so valuable that she may be sought by potential suitors, but she still has be won on the battlefield of love.

The "B" clause of verse 10 suggests that she can't be bought, for her price is far above rubies. This kind of woman doesn't need or want a sugar daddy, but she desires a life partner to join her success with his. Understand again that this life partner is not a long-term living together companion but her husband.

In the previous chapter, I told you that the virtuous woman is not interested in dishonorable relationships that detract from her noble image. So, she is not a woman who needs a man in her life who is not her husband to make her feel valuable. In fact, she quickly ends any relationship with anyone who does not seriously consider marriage other than casual friendships. The truly virtuous woman knows that the man doesn't make her valuable but she understands that she is valuable long before she meets him.

So many women today remain in relationships with men that are clearly not going anywhere, and they stay in these relationships on the man's terms. They are clearly not going to marry these women; they see these women only when they want to see them. And a lot of them won't even give the children who are born in these relationships their last name.

For years, I've wondered why women stay in these kinds of relationships with men that devalue them. Then it became clear that a lot of women attach their value and their sense of self-worth to having a man in their life. That also gave me some insight as to why some women get involved with married men, having relationships that last for years in some cases. It's because they have somehow justified the idea that a piece of a man is better than no man at all even if they have to share him—even if the piece they have is just sexual.

'VALUABLE TO HER HUSBAND'

This woman is valuable in three very basic but crucial areas: her relationship with her husband; in her relationship with her family (i.e., children); and last but not least, her community. Let's take a look at the first of these areas of her value.

> **The heart of her husband doth safely trust in her, so that he shall have no need of spoil. (KJV, Prov. 31:11)**

This verse makes it clear that the virtuous woman is valuable to her husband. The Bible declares that "the heart of her husband does safely trust in her."

Notice, if you will, the use of the word "safely" in the phrase. It denotes certainty, surety, and an absence of doubt in her. That simply means that he completely trusts her, and there is nothing that he would withhold from her. Now, if you have or ever had someone in which you could completely trust in, then you know how valuable that kind of person can be to you. That kind of person is truly a Godsend because you can confide in that person your innermost secrets.

I need to make it clear that people don't really know you until they know your secrets. Now the person who knows your secrets is the person who really knows the real you. Therefore, material possessions never become an obstacle in the relationship because they have entrusted their emotional treasure to each other, which is attached to their secrets. Yes, the sharing of your secrets helps the other person know you better, which in turn allows them to love you—all of you.

Think about it, what makes a relationship sour? When you can no longer trust the other person. And why can you no longer trust? Because he (or she) began lying to you. Why did he (or she) lie? Because there is something one person didn't want the other person to know. Thus, what is a lie? It's an attempt to conceal a secret. Concealing secrets makes you feel like you don't really know the other person. Therefore, you can't truly love what you don't know.

What's the real treasure of a relationship? What's the one thing that the other person probably can't hide from anyone else but you? Is it money or possessions? No, those things can be obtained from other places. There may be people whom you might share your money and things with, but not your secrets.

Now, the failure to be transparent with each other may cause one of you to feel as though you don't know that person, and therefore you should not trust him (or her). That could lead you to withholding material possessions, trust, or love. But when this level of trust and love exists in a relationship, it allows both the woman and the man an opportunity to wholly love and be a blessing to each other. So much so that the Bible says that "her husband shall have no need of spoil."

When I speak of the sharing of secrets, I mean that there should be no secrets between a husband and wife. I think it also needs to be said many of these secrets should have been shared during the premarital stage of the relationship. This would allow both an opportunity to know what they may be getting into. I'm not suggesting that either party just freely volunteer any information because there maybe things that the other person doesn't want to know. But, if the question is asked, one should be honest in his (or her) response, or at least honest as one is ready to be at the time. Remember, this is the one person you never want to think of you as a liar.

The Message Bible says something to the effect that "he will never have to regret his trust in her." Now that kind of certainty comes from not withholding anything from her. He has no regrets because she has been both good to him and good for him. How is she good to him you might ask?

Here's what verse 12 says about her goodness to him:

> "She will do him good and not evil all the days of her life."
> (KJV, Prov. 31:12)

The King James Version says "she's going to be good to him and not evil to him." The verse implies that she is going to be an aid to him and not an enemy; an asset, not a liability. She's not working against him, but she's working *with* him in an attempt to build a life together.

Look at how that same verse reads in the Living Bible Translation.

> "She will not hinder him but help all her life." (LBT, Prov. 31:12)

This translation further affirms that she is an asset to her husband, and she is not only helpful but supportive. One of the things that both men and women crave is someone who believes in them and their dreams, no matter how far fetched they are. One of the worst things that can happen in a relationship is when the other person becomes your dream killer. But the real tragedy of this is the person whose dream was killed never dreams again. But the virtuous woman is no dream killer; she is a dream supporter. She does whatever she can to help it come to pass in the life of her husband, because she knows that within the success of his dreams lies the success of her own and those of her children.

Now, I said she was both good to him and good for him, and here's how she's good for him:

> "Her husband is known in the gates, when he sitteth among the elders of the land." (KJV, Prov. 31:23)

The text seems to imply that because of her, her husband has gained the respect of the leaders of his community because he is both known and seated among the elders. Its one thing to be known among the elders because you could be known as a troublemaker, or as someone with a bad reputation. Those kinds of things can get you known among the elders, but it doesn't make you respectable. But to be seated among them is significant, because it says that you are of like character and stature. And why is he there? The virtuous woman in his life has been both good to him and for him.

'VALUABLE TO HER FAMILY'

She is not only valuable to her husband but to her family (i.e., children) as well. Here's what verse 15 has to say about her.

> "She looketh well to the ways of her household, and eateth not the bread of idleness." (KJV, Prov. 31:15)

This is a woman who has a strong sense of family and does what is necessary to develop a strong healthy family. Look at what she does to ensure that the family is not without even if she has to work day and night to secure it. The text suggests that the woman is not lazy in maintaining her family. But when you read the verse in the Living Bible Translation it reveals something much deeper about her:

> "She carefully watches all that goes on in her household
> and does not have to bear the consequences of laziness."
> (LBT, Prov. 31:27)

It points out that this woman is busy parenting and supervising. She keeps a careful eye on her children and all that goes on around them. She is even mindful of the people around them. She doesn't allow the television, radio, computer, or even anyone other than herself to raise her children. She understands that there are things out there that she does not want her children being exposed to.

This virtuous woman also knows that children are very impressionable, and most of their core values are obtained in the home. She also knows that there are things that only she should impart into her kids—not the television, some other person, or even for that matter another family member. She understands the delicate and complex relationship between a mother and her children, and she realizes that the window of opportunity to solidify it is limited. So, she seizes every opportunity she can.

Virtue and wisdom tells her that she must model what she wants her children to become. How does she do it, you might ask? Here's how: She monitors what her children watch on television by watching it with them or by checking it out to ensure that program is suitable for them.

In so many homes, the television has become the parent. I don't think that I need to say that television isn't what it used to be. Television producers used to have as an aim of their programming the promotion of good, wholesome family values. But if you've turned your television on lately you know that there are shows that are neither good nor wholesome. So, the virtuous woman makes sure that what her children watch meets her standards, and most importantly godly standards.

But she doesn't stop there. She takes it a step further. The virtuous woman understands that part of being a parent to her children may require the sacrificing of personal ambitions until her children reach a stage of self-sufficiency; her responsibility is to get them there.

Do you remember what the Bible said about Hannah and the rearing of her son Samuel?

> (21). And now the man Elkanah and all his house, went to offer unto the Lord the yearly sacrifice, and his vow. (22). But Hannah went not up; for she said unto her husband, I will not go up until the child be weaned, and then I will bring him, that he may appear before the Lord, and there abide forever. (KJV, I Sam. 1:21-22)

Nobody had more reason than Hannah to go and offer up sacrifices at Shiloh. After all, the Lord had given her a child as she had prayed for. But the Bible says that Hannah did not go. She instinctively knew that the child came first and her husband told her to do what felt right to her.

What I'm simply saying is that a woman of virtue should feel right about her decision to put her child(ren) first. The child didn't ask for you; you asked for the child.

Furthermore, she is a provider of her child's needs right along with the man whose role should be both father and husband. The following verses bear witness to this:

> "She riseth also while it is yet night, and giveth meat to her house-hold, and a portion to her handmaidens." (KVJ, Prov.31:15)

> "She is not afraid of the snow for her household: For all of her household are clothed with scarlet." (KJV, Prov. 31:21)

These verses show that she provides both food and clothing for her children, a safe environment to be reared in, and the support of a loving mother. But there is something else as it pertains to family.

Verse 28 shows that her efforts are not in vain but that they are appreciated by the entire family.

> "Her children arise up, and call her blessed; her husband also, and he praiseth her." (KJV, Prov. 31:28)

And as you probably know, one of the most valuable assets in the lives of children is the loving support of their mother.

'VALUABLE TO HER COMMUNITY'

Now, you're probably wondering that after being valuable to her husband and to her family, the virtuous woman could not have much energy left to be of any value to her community. But she is valuable to her community, and you'll also be surprised to know that she achieves much of this value through what she does with her husband and family: She ensures the family unit remains strong. Thus, she strengthens the community.

Let's take a look at how she does it.

By being valuable to her husband she blesses the community. The community now has another respectable elder and leader that it did not have, adding to the stability of it. They also add to the community additional role models and teachers for which it to draw from.

Take a look at what is also gained by a virtuous woman's value to her family (i.e., children). By being valuable to her family, she gets the opportunity to reshape her community by providing morally strong leaders of the future.

How do her children accomplish this? The virtuous woman exemplifies the morals and standards that she's taught them. They are likely to have a strong sense of God and family, and they understand the sanctity of marriage.

Now, some might ask is this of any value to the community? The answer to that question is a resounding "yes." They are both interrelated. In other words, as the family goes so goes the community. If you ask any sociologist who is worth his/her salt they will tell you that the community is a larger model of what the family essentially has become.

A large part of the problem within our communities is the breakdown of the family. What becomes acceptable in the family almost automatically becomes socially acceptable to the community. Family and community are inextricably linked together. But there are other ways the virtuous woman is valuable to her community that Proverbs 31 points out.

> "She riseth also while it is yet night, and giveth meat to her household, and a portion to her maidens." (KVJ, Prov. 31:15)

This woman is not just of good standing in her community, but the "C" clause of verse 15 shows that she is a financial asset to her community, because she's an employer.

She has handmaids that are in her employ and under her supervision as well. She adds to the community's economy by providing jobs to those who live in it. In short, she has a keen sense for business and she is a respected businesswoman who runs her operations with integrity. But there's still more to this woman that is of value to her community.

> "She considereth a field, and buyeth it: with the fruit of her hands she planteth a vineyard." (KJV, Prov. 31:16)

Not only is she an economic asset to the community, she's also an economic developer. Notice the scripture says "she considers a field." To me, it says she has vision because that's what she's doing by considering it. By considering it, she envisions it as more than what it is. She makes her community better off by bringing the best out of it.

The Bible teaches us a few things about this virtuous woman that we all should know. But the one thing it teaches us above all is that women who have virtue are valuable. And that value extends far beyond her: it enriches the relationship between her and her husband, her family and even the relationship she has with her community.

I also think that we should remember that her value is not derived by just being a woman, but it comes from the virtue that she displays.

CHAPTER 4

Virtuous Women Are Hard to Find

_____

One of the questions I am often asked by both the women of the church that I've been privileged to pastor and by women abroad as I travel is where are all the good men and how do I get one?

My reply is usually "there are plenty of good men out there, and the way you get one is to let him find you." To which they respond, "I'm not hard to find."

Now, while that comeback may seem comical to some degree according to Proverbs 31:10, it's not all together truthful. Do you recall what that tenth verse says? Let's look at it in several different translations pay careful attention to the "A" clause of each:

> Who can find a virtuous woman? For her price is far above rubies. (KJV, Prov. 31: 10)

> A capable wife who can find? She is far more precious than jewels. (New Revised Standard Version, Prov. 31: 10)

> Who can find a virtuous and capable wife? She is worth more that precious rubies. (New Living Translation, Prov. 31: 10)

> A good woman is hard to find, and her worth is far more than diamonds. (Message Bible, Prov. 31:10)

As you read these translations of Proverbs 31:10, it becomes increasingly clear that King Lemuel's mother is telling him that the kind of woman who would make him a good wife is a rare find. In fact, when you read the "A" clause of verse 10, the Message Bible states outright that a good woman is hard to find.

Now here is where I may loose some of my female readers. It's because I'm sure some of you may take issue with what I'm about to say. Proverbs 31:10 makes it clear that not only are good men hard to find, but sadly so are women.

If you keep in mind the timeline of when the book of Proverbs was written, you'll come to the realization that this short supply of good women is not by any means a new phenomenon. It's a very old and present reality in the world we live in.

That's right, my sister, there is also a shortage of good women. Now, it didn't say that there was a shortage of women; that's not the case. However, not all women should be considered virtuous by Proverbs 31 standards. And if there is any place that needs to exemplify this more than any other it has to be the church.

Let's take a look at the church. In almost every church in America on almost any given Sunday about seventy-five percent of the congregation is female. And of this majority that comprises the Body of Christ, few are women that King Lemuel's mother would consider to be or a good woman (virtuous).

Why, you might ask?

It's because so many of us have been taught the Church Girl Principle: the common belief that women who attend church are good women (virtuous). But that principle simply just does not hold true in many cases.

The major problem with this principle is that location does not make a woman virtuous or a man holy, nor does money, position, birth, or clothing. Virtue does not come from where you are, what you wear, what your title is, or even what your name is, but it's what you do. Because whatever you do is really who you are; and therefore, what you are.

For example, if you steal you are a thief; if you cheat you are a cheater; and if you lie then what you really are is a liar. In other words, what I'm saying is that your lifestyle determines what you really are, and that's what virtue really is: a way of life.

If we took a close and an honest look at the body of Christ (the church) we would have to say that the lives among the majority of us who make up the body of Christ, their hearts are far away from Christ in the way we live our lives. And because women make up such a large majority of the church it is even more visible in them—not that the men of the church are any closer to God in the way that they live.

There are many examples of women living morally unhealthy and unholy lives in the church without knowing the depth of emotional and spiritual damage they are doing to themselves.

DOOMING A RELATIONSHIP TO FAILURE

Let's look at two kinds of lifestyles that cause all kinds of emotional and spiritual damage in the women who live them. One of the things that couples today are doing more than ever is living together before marriage. Perhaps this is more popular now because you see it everywhere and it seems as though everybody is doing it.

Look at Hollywood and all of the live-in romances, and let's not have a discussion about what is seen on television or at the movies. You can hardly watch anything now without it being centered on some couple living together without being married.

Years ago, this kind of lifestyle was frowned upon and the people who led this kind of lifestyle hid it from everyone because they were ashamed of it. Now it is seen as acceptable and decent. In fact, many indulge in it to safeguard against divorce because somehow they have rationalized that they can workout any potential problems in the impending marriage by living together. But instead of safeguarding against divorce it actually secures it.

Studies show couples who live together before marriage can expect failure. The divorce rate for these couples is significantly higher. Here are the numbers: In H. Norman Wright's *Finding Your Perfect Mate* he writes, "Out of 100 couples that live together before marriage, [forty] of them will break up and never get married at all; of the [sixty] who get married [thirty-five] of them will divorce . . . that leaves only [twenty-five] out of the original 100 who will make it."

When you crunch the numbers it becomes even more frightening and alarming for those who really want their marriage to succeed. According to Wright, the bottom line is that couples who live together before marriage have a twenty-five percent chance of making it work. But let's not forget about the forty percent of couples who live together before marriage never making it to the altar.

I know. You're already saying but we're different and we're in that twenty-fifth percentile that's going to make it. But that's easier said than done; the numbers don't lie. Many couples who enter into these kinds of living arrangements are in denial that divorce is a possibility. But it's far more than just a possibility. It's a reality in most cases.

What most couples don't realize is that living with someone

isn't like trying out for the basketball team and hoping you'll make it. It's not even like going on a job interview for the job you've been hoping for. You don't try out for the role of the husband or wife for some production. You can only *become* either of these roles when you *are* them.

It's like trying to find out what it is like to be pregnant without being pregnant. You will never know how that feels unless you are pregnant. The same could be said about living in a married person's environment without being married. It does not tell you how marriage is going to be nor does it help you make a potential marriage successful.

Norman also says, "Living with someone before marriage clouds one's judgment and they make irrational decisions that are not objective when they look at problem areas."

'THE TEST FACTOR'

The major factor why living together before marriage doesn't work is a little thing I like to call "The Test Factor."

In other words, when two people are living together without the benefit of marriage they can never and will never get it out of their minds that this is only a test. They are constantly aware that they're not really married to the other person; therefore, they shouldn't commit themselves completely to this arrangement or the other person. They can never quite completely give themselves over to the other person no matter how much they love them and no matter how long they've lived together in that arrangement.

Why is that the case, you may ask?

An arrangement is not the same as a covenant, no matter how much they want the arrangement they entered into be recognized. There are no guarantees in those living arrangements because all that you really have is the word of the other person. And sometimes they just simply change their mind.

The reason they are in an unendurable arrangement is because you have nothing to hold the other person to other than what he or she said, and the Bible describes man's words as unpredictable and unreliable.

Now, here's the thing that we really need to just come to grips with, and that is none of us fully trust an individual according to their word alone no matter who they are. Although we may profess to have trust in certain people, there is probably nobody we trust in completely simply because man will at some point let you down, whether intentionally or unintentionally.

When things become rough-and-tumble in a living together arrangement you really have no one to blame but yourself. You can blame the other person, but you knew when you entered into that arrangement that they were unpredictable. And to be quite honest, you really can't blame God because you took God out of the equation when you entered into that arrangement.

There is nothing about a living together arrangement that is godly. In fact, when you read the Bible, there's not much in there about living together without the benefit of marriage.

Furthermore, there is not much in the Bible on boyfriends and girlfriends. But there is a wealth of knowledge on living together as husbands and wives, because that's God's will for his people. When you read the first three chapters from the book of Genesis you will find that God never intended for man to live together without being married because God refers to Eve as Adam's wife, not his girlfriend. Even when God's people were in captivity, He said to His people, "Marry and have sons and daughters, and find wives for your sons and give your daughter in marriage." (New King James, Jer. 29:6)

So, what I'm really trying to say is that there is no precedent for that kind of relationship in the Word of God, and ultimately no excuse for it in the world today. It doesn't matter how much you try to justify it, there's no excuse.

Okay, so you've been living like this for a long time. Well it's never too late to get out. Maybe it's the way your whole family has lived their lives. But the cycle has to be broken by someone—why not you?

If it's out of convenience and it's just easier, then remember the road to hell is also convenient, because sin is always easier than doing it right.

Perhaps it's a money problem and you need financial assistance. God says He will supply all of your financial needs. Maybe you just need the companionship of another person. God says He is a friend that sticks closer than a brother. Not only that, God will send the right person into your life at the right time, and it won't be just a boyfriend or a girlfriend. It will be the wife or husband just as He has willed for you, His people.

POISONING A RELATIONSHIP

The other lifestyle that is also very detrimental to a relationship—and will in most cases lead to its doom and failure—is when you engage in sexual activity without the benefit of marriage.

Let me say in the onset that I am not saying that there is anything wrong with sex. Sex is a beautiful thing and Lord knows we all like it and enjoy it even those of us who publicly pretend not to have an appetite for it. But sex has to be practiced in the proper context, a married context. After all that was God's original intended practice. Remember what it notes in the book of Genesis:

> And Adam knew Eve his wife; and she conceived, and bare Cain, and said, I have gotten a man from the Lord. (KJV, Gen. 4:1)

Please keep in mind that this text occurs after the fall of man because after that event sex takes on a new component. Prior to the fall of man, sex served the purpose of consummating the marriage between man and woman and as a bonding agent to join that man and his wife together. But after the fall, God added a new component to sex between man and wife, procreation.

Until that point, God Himself served as sole creator of human life having created Adam and Eve with His own hands and having breathed the breath of life into their nostrils. After their fall, God incorporated man into that process without changing the original context and purpose of sex. Some may argue that sex between Adam and Eve, including myself in times past, did not take place until Gen. 4:1 when Cain was conceived. But conception of a child does not define nor determine a sexual encounter because not every sexual encounter leads to conception.

I should also note that when sex took place for the first time it was ordained by God, and it took place between a husband and a wife. If practiced in this context between husband and wife, sex can be not only beautiful, explosive, and intoxicating, but a whole lot of other things can also become a blessing to the marital union.

However, if sex is practiced outside of a marital context, as beautiful as it maybe, it can be like poison to any relationship that doesn't have the benefit of a marital covenant.

Think about it. How many relationships have you been in that looked promising right up until it became sexual?

THE SPOILED MILK PRINCIPLE

Relationships are almost like milk. It tastes good and looks good. And if I can borrow from the Dairy Farmers' Association, it does the body good. But if you take that same milk and pour a little vinegar in it, the milk spoils immediately and goes bad.

That's the way relationships work. They are in many ways just milk. A relationship can be very good in appearance, meaning that you both look good together. Not only that, he or she can be the right kind of person you're supposed to be with. Allow me to agree with the dairy farmers that this kind of relationship can do your body good. That's because good relationships can be like medicine to your body, especially those that are stress-free, supportive, and nurturing. But no matter how good the relationship is, it only takes a little vinegar to spoil it. That's what sex does—it spoils it.

Sex is to non-marital relationships what vinegar is to good, wholesome milk. It spoils whatever it comes in contact with, and it literally poisons the milk of your relationship, if instituted and practiced.

The reason it poisons a relationship is because it changes everything. What vinegar does to milk is change the color, taste, and the milk's consistency. The truth is that vinegar changes whole milk into something that is akin to buttermilk in taste, color, and consistency.

Now, buttermilk may make good biscuits, pancakes, and waffles; however, butter by itself is almost good for nothing. In fact, too much buttermilk can make a person sick by leading to all types of health problem like high cholesterol, clogged arteries, and hypertension. Coincidentally, all these illnesses can lead to heart trouble and, yes, even heart failure.

I suspect that some of you are already saying that I just agreed with the dairy farmers' catchphrase that milk does the body good. And you're saying to yourself that it's still the same milk. I submit to you that it's not the same milk. Something else has been introduced to it that wasn't there before. And that "something" has changed what used to be good for you into something that could kill you.

Why, you might ask?

Because it changed that milk into something that was totally different from what once was. What changed it? Vinegar was the only thing that was added. And that's what happens to a relation-ship when you add sex before marriage: it changes it into some-thing that is all together different than what it was.

That's right. A healthy, wholesome relationship will be spoiled by the poison of sex before marriage. And what was once palat-able to your emotional taste buds is now repulsive because sex changed the taste of it. The shinning white gleam of our once milky white relationship is now yellowed by sex and it has dark-ened the future of the relationship because sex has changed the color of the relationship.

Finally, the relationship that was once smooth and flowing has now become a quagmire because sex has changed the consistency of the relationship. And the same thing that once brought you pleasure now is the source of your greatest pain. What once made you laugh now makes you cry and, yes, what once brought you life may now be slowly killing you.

Therefore, let us be careful not to taint the milk of a potentially good relationship with premarital sex. A sure-fire way to do that from this point forward is to think about how many times God may have answered your prayers for that help meet, husband, wife, and soulmate, but we out of our selfish desires poisoned the milk of what might have been a God-sent relationship to the ex-tent that we're no longer able to drink it.

CHAPTER 5

Why Won't He Marry Me?

question that I've found commonly asked among women is, "Why Won't He Marry Me?" So many of these women are frustrated and fed up in relationships that for as far as they can see aren't going anywhere, and they've gone nowhere for quite a while.

In many cases, these women sit around to wait on these men hand-and-foot, thinking that they can get him to marry them by their service. They sadly learn that these men simply will not marry them no matter what she's done for him.

There are many reasons why men don't marry certain women, but they usually stem from one of four basic reasons: a) Some men are just users; b) Some men are afraid to love; c) Some men are afraid of commitment; d) Some men are afraid to commit because of the fear of failure.

Let's take a closer look at the reasons and delve into the psyche of the men who exhibit these behaviors. Take into account that much of what has been written about men who won't marry or love has been written by women who have written out of their experiences with men; therefore, they write from a woman's perspective. But I believe in order to fully understand why this behavior occurs and in many cases reoccurs in men, we must get into the psyche of a man. And what better way to do that than to have a man share his thinking on this behavior.

SOME MEN ARE JUST USERS

I guess the best way to begin this discussion is to go ahead, get the embarrassing confession out of the way, and admit that what women have been saying about men is true. But that's only true about some men, thank God.

Now, being a man myself, it is embarrassing to admit that some of us men, to borrow a phase from my father in one of his many talks to me about being a man, "ain't worth a dime." In fact, they aren't men. They're just males, and it is possible to be a male and still not be a man.

That's because real men understand and accept a little thing my daddy called responsibility. Therefore, any male who calls himself a man and does not both understand and accept responsibility, but yet goes around proclaiming to be a man, is no man at all. He is an imposter.

Real men aren't just males. They're much more than that. They're "male" men. That's right, and they know how and do deliver.

Real men view the women in their lives as their responsibility and they want to be an asset rather than a liability. At least that is what real men do in the life of the woman they love. But there are some imposters out there who get involved with women and aren't men at all. They are just males pretending to be men.

Now, my sisters, when you meet these imposters don't be fooled by what comes out of their mouths, because they talk a

In fact instead of adding to you, all they ever really do is take from you because they are always so needy.

That's right, I said needy.

They need a place to stay. They need you to feed them. They need to drive your car. They need your credit card(s). They need you to buy their clothes. They need you to finance their lifestyle as a high roller. They need you to baby sit their kids and deal with the women who bore them for him. They need you to believe in them, encourage them, support them, and the list just goes on and on. And what do you get in exchange for these goods and services? Perhaps a few fleeting moments of private pleasure.

Maybe you aren't one of those women dealing with this kind of man, yet there are thousands of women who are. What they need to do is find a piece of paper and pen, sit down, and draw a line down the middle of the paper. On one side, write down everything that they've both given and done for the man in their life. On the other side, write down everything they've received in return from the man. (Oh, by the way, promises don't count. Only what he has delivered and is delivering.)

After having done this, sit back for a moment and take a good look at both sides. Ask yourself if he is adding enough to you to justify his presence in your life. This process can sometimes be a painful one simply because there are times when we just fall in love with some people who are just worthless.

But this process is sure to do two very important things: a) It will properly identify if the man in your life is in fact a man or just an imposter; b) It will almost certainly erase any doubt about your decision to dismiss him from your life because he's been worthless and/or he's not adding to you.

This should also help you to move on and settle the question of what if. When you've done this simple evaluation and have gotten out of that unbalanced relationship, it's only then that you will see that relationship never added to you but took away from you. It won't be until you see it in black and white that you will finally accept the fact that what you thought was helping you was actually holding you back—the facts just don't lie.

Some Men are Afraid to Love

Here is an all too common and little known fact about men: some are afraid to love.

Yes, that's right, afraid to love.

This is by far, in my opinion, a major contributing factor as to why most men won't and never get married. I know that this may come as a shock to many of you, because men more often than not won't admit it, but men get hurt and emotionally scarred in relationships, too.

Keep in mind, that this is perfectly normal; and as sure as you live and love, you're also going to lose in love. And I don't think I have to tell you that losing something you love is always painful, especially when the thing is a person. That's why we morn at the death of a love one. Because although we know what the Bible says about those who die in the Lord, it still does not change the fact that we have lost them on this side of glory.

The most important thing is not why we grieve but the fact that the grieving has taken place. That's the thing that men don't do when they lose at love. Most men have been raised not to grieve over anything because outward displays of emotion are seen as weakness, and that it makes them less of a man. But men lose the one thing that grieving has to offer them by trying to preserve this macho manly image: Reconciliation.

When we grieve over the loss of a thing, no matter what it is, it forces us to have to admit that what we've lost is gone, and that we somehow have to find a way to live life without it. It is through our grieving that we reach a point of reconciling whether we're going to live life looking back at what we've lost or we're going to live life facing forward and having to live life without it.

In other words, grieving leads us toward reconciling what we've lost in order for us to move on and get past it. This is an underlying reason why many men are afraid to love. It's because they have failed to reconcile the grief of a lost relationship and they can't move on to the next one because they're haunted by the pain of the one they lost.

A man who is afraid to love is afraid because he can't bear the thought of experiencing what he's experienced once before, and he also knows that to get involved in another relationship is to allow someone else to be close enough to wound him again. So, what he does is make the decision that, no matter what, he's not going to fall in love again. To fall in love with someone is to expose one's heart to somebody who maybe holding a dagger, waiting on a moment to strike a potentially fatal blow.

Now, understand that this man does not stop dealing with women; he just won't fall in love with one. He'll be friends with them, work with them, go out in public with them, and wine and dine them. He'll still live with them and, yes, even sleep with them. But he will not, by any means, love them. In fact, if he feels himself falling for the woman, he will break off all contact with her.

Why?

Because he's made up his mind never to be hurt again even if it means him becoming the person who does the hurting. But what he doesn't realize is the same decision he's made never to love has positioned him never to be loved in return.

He has forgotten that love is like a two-lane highway and not a one-way street. In other words, for him to receive love he has to give love. Thus, until he reconciles the pain of his past relationship(s) that broke his heart he will always be afraid to love. Nor will he be in a position to be healed and made whole.

It is in finding the courage to move on from painful relationships by reconciling our grief, admitting that it's over, and pressing forward into life and new relationships that we find the thing which heals us from our past pain and makes us whole again.

Someone once said time heals all wounds. But I submit that time alone cannot heal the wounds of a broken heart.

Time, in this case, must be coupled with love.

Some Men Are Afraid of Commitment

Here's another reason why men won't marry. It's something that women have been saying for years: Some men are afraid to commit.

Yes, that's right, ladies, a man is finally admitting it. Commitment scares some of us. And some of us can't handle what commitment brings along with it: Accountability.

These men are afraid of commitment simply because they know that committing to someone requires that they become accountable to the person that they have committed themselves to. Because when you're in a relationship with someone, if that relationship is to be successful, both people in the relationship must see themselves as accountable to each other. That requires that your thinking and your methods of doing things must change, and they have to change from a singular perception to a dual perception.

That's right. You have to consider the other person in everything that you do, or even purpose to do. When committing yourself to someone, you have to settle in your mind there is no more I, but us; and no more me, but we.

Now, there are essentially two reasons why men seem to have a fear of commitment: Either they just don't want to be accountable, or they are afraid of failing.

Let's take a look at these two basic reasons men fear commitment:

Here's what you need to keep in mind as we look at the first of these two reasons why men fear commitment, and that is that some men are not willing to be held accountable. Now, while there are men out there who have a problem with accountability to women, most men have no problem holding a woman accountable to them.

Think about it. No matter how irresponsible some men are in their relationship to their spouse or girlfriend about their time, money, or whereabouts, these are the ones who seem to demand accountability from the woman.

They want to know where she is, where she's been, and what time she's coming home. Yet these same men take issue with being asked when he's coming home or whether he came home at all from the previous night.

This man wants to know how much she was paid, when she bought that dress, and what she's done with her money. He wants to know this whether he gives her any money or whether he pays or doesn't pay any of the bills in the house. Many of these men have no problem holding the woman in their life accountable, yet many of them cannot tolerate being accountable to a woman for the same reasons they demanded accountability from her.

At the same time, they have no problem being accountable to the people they work for at the job, on the community board, or the people in their fraternity. That same accountability, however, is missing in action at home.

Why is this?

To a lot of men, being accountable to the woman in his life is seen as being weak and unmanly. For example, to some, calling home if he's going to be late might be contrived as being hen pecked. The truth is that this common courtesy is not a cause for feeling unmanly or hen pecked. It actually conveys responsibility and consideration for the other person. And when an individual is willing to be held accountable to the other person in that relationship, it shows that this individual is responsible and can be trusted.

Along those same lines, if you haven't figured it out by now, trust never binds you, but it frees you, so much that after you've gained someone's trust they don't want or need to know where you've been. There is confidence in knowing wherever you've been is all right because they know you are trustworthy.

FEAR OF FAILURE

There's also the man who fears commitment because he fears he's going to fail either because he has failed before, or because the men in his life have failed miserably at it. Therefore, when you ask him to commit to a relationship, he almost immediately retreats from it as though it was a plague.

It's always fairly easy to spot these men because whenever the relationship reaches a point of seriousness that requires a decision to be made whether they'll take the relationship any further or discontinue it, this man almost always chooses to end the relationship.

There's really nothing abnormal about that decision. But it's the way he chooses to end the relationship that makes it kind of strange. Instead of sitting down with the other person in the relationship and convey his feelings, he'll simply leave without warning, having almost disappeared from the face of the earth. So the woman is then left feeling lonely, abandoned, and wondering what happened to what seemed like a promising relationship between the two of them.

Now why does this man end the relationship so abruptly? Is it because he fears he's going to fail her, he's become so attached to her, and he really doesn't want to take her through any emotional turmoil with him in a committed relationship with him?

Quite possibly, he does this because he's often aware of something awry about himself. Sadly, in his attempt to save her some future heartache, he ends up hurting her in the abrupt manner the relationship ends.

Many times the man flees the relationship because he feels the woman deserves somebody better than him. He might feel that way because of unresolved issues in his own life that he knows are bound to make this potential relationship rocky.

Keep in mind that these issues could be almost anything. It could be that he has a problem with fidelity and he is incapable of being faithful to the woman even after he's committed to her. Maybe he has a gambling, drinking, or drug addiction that he is still battling and he knows that his addiction is still stronger than his commitment to the woman in his life. Or believe it or not, it might even stem from relationships that had nothing to do with him, but those that he saw while growing up.

As a result, he feels that the same bad qualities he saw modeled in other men like a father, uncle, grandfather, brother or even a mentor, are somehow apart of him. He feels that he is no better than these men, and because of this he feels that he is doomed or destined to make the same painful mistakes that he saw them make and hurt the women in their lives. So he runs from commitment not because he doesn't want it or doesn't love the woman, but because he can't quite bring himself up to do it.

There are many possible reasons why the man will not or men in your life have not committed. But if you're curious about pinpointing the issue or issues—since there can be multiple issues—get to know him, the men in his life, and inquire about or listen to his past life experiences. By combining these elements with your rationale and understanding, you will discover who he is and how he's become what he is.

CHAPTER 6

The Maturity of Virtue

No doubt, the virtuous woman is to be praised as Proverbs 31:30 proclaims. But the virtuous woman is not only a woman who lives her life disciplined by the wisdom of the Word of God.

Time shows us that she's much more. For like a bottle of fine wine, she gets better and more valuable with age. It is of the utmost importance that we realize we are all getting older and not younger.

Although you live a life of virtue, many in this world do not. Not only have many in this life forsaken the principles of virtue, but also morality, justice, and the Golden Rule of Luke 6:31. For truly in this life regardless of our walk with God we will suffer many things from many people.

Jesus preached that we would have tribulation. But as a woman of virtue, much like grapes that hang on the vine and endure the heat of day, the cold of night, wind, rain, dust, and time, all that you endure makes you better and not bitter.

Much like those grapes that endure the test of time, they are transformed into a finer and more valuable wine to be relished and savored by those who drink it. So is the woman of virtue transformed with age.

Titus 2 gives us some insight into her transformation. He tells us that with age the woman of virtue is transformed into a powerful and insightful teacher and instructor. The KJV of the Bible in Titus 2:3 the last clause of that verse says that the aged women are to be "teachers of good things."

The Apostle Paul instructs Titus to teach the older women to teach the young women, but he also reminds Titus to tell them that their instruction to the young women will only be as powerful as their example.

Look at the "B" clause of verse 3, "that they be in behavior as becomes holiness."

The apostle makes it clear to us that it's hard to effectively teach that which we do not live. But it is also clear from this passage that example is by far the best teacher. Hence, it should be our desire to be Christ-like—to emulate or follow His example.

Exemplification was also Jesus' manner of instruction. Remember Luke's opening statement in the book of Acts 1:1 :

> **"The former treatise have I made, O Theophilus, of all that Jesus began both to do and teach." (KJV, Acts 1:1)**

The text shows us that not only was Jesus a divine teacher, but also that much, if not all, that Jesus taught was by example. I have often had to admit to my congregation that some things from the Word of God that I've taught them were things I had to wait to teach them.

I had to wait to teach it until I could live it because the life you live is stronger than any sermon you can preach overcomes any oratory skills you may have, and it lasts longer than any lesson you can teach.

Jesus knew the power of words spoken by men who live them, that's why John 6:63 quotes Him saying, "[T]he words that I speak unto you, they are spirit and they are life." The life that we lead either pours life into others or drains life out of them. Its why no words of wisdom can compare to the power of an exemplified life. Living a life of obedience to God adds weight to our words, qualifies our witness, and draws others to God.

I believe that King Lemeul's mother spoke of this value in a woman of virtue:

> "Who can find a virtuous woman? For her price is far above rubies." (KJV, Prov. 31:10)

The Apostle Paul also makes clear that this value can not only be attributed to time alone, but time has to be coupled with a life connected to God and the wisdom of His Word.

There are many people in the world who have lived many years, but they show little wisdom; they just get old. There's never any real change in their lives except for a few physical limitations brought on by age. They're basically who they've always been.

Although they've aged, they still live being controlled by the flesh and still pursuing the lust of their flesh, doing what feels good to them rather than what's right. So, not every aged woman is qualified to be an instructor of young women. Paul even went as far as to point out those that are "false accusers and drink too much wine."

The apostle tells young women to stay away from old women who gossip and drink too much. Because what you do is just as important, if not more important, as what you teach.

Nobody buys wine from a cab driver or a mechanic simply because that's not what they do. Just as anyone who appreciates great wine knows to seek out the older bottles in the cellar that they might savor and enjoy flavor and smoothness that only time can produce. Therefore, young women must seek out what the mature, godly woman of virtue possesses.

THE LOVE LESSONS

There are two important lessons that the older godly women should teach the young: to love their husbands and to love their children. These lessons seem like two areas where basic instincts and common sense should prevail. But the lessons that the mature woman of virtue teaches the young has little or nothing to do with the command to love, but rather it has everything to do with how to love the husband and children.

Although the how to's of love may seem like common sense and second nature, most people struggle with how to love. When we really think about it, falling in love is the easy part. In fact, we do it without realizing it.

Think about it, you never realize that you're falling in love until you've already fallen. The act of falling in love happens so smoothly and swiftly that its only recognized in the aftermath. So, instruction about falling in love is pretty much superfluous; it's kind of like teaching a baby to blink or breathe. But what requires instruction is the expression of that which we've fallen into.

When a woman falls in love with a man and him with her, that event may lead them into marriage. After the sparks stop flying and the earth stops spinning, the two of them must get down to the business of love.

That requires consistent acts of expression on the part of each person. This is the part of love between a husband and wife that needs instruction—many people just don't know how to express their love for the other person in a manner that honors and makes the other person feel secure.

I believe this was the Apostle Paul's intent when he says to the men, "Husbands, love your wives, even as Christ loved the church, and gave himself for it." (KJV, Eph. 5:25)

Likewise, Paul instructs the women, "Wives submit yourselves unto your own husbands, as unto the Lord." (KJV, Eph. 5:23).

This was Paul's attempt at showing us that instruction is needed for love, and it was also his attempt to instruct us in the act of loving one another. This is the duty Paul instructs Titus to pass on to the older women of virtue—that they teach younger women how to love their husbands and children.

There are many things that can be done to express love to a husband and child, and I'm sure many basic and practical acts come to mind. But Paul instructed Titus that the older women of the church should teach the younger women.

He suggested there were five areas that are most crucial in the expression of love from wife to husband and from mother to children:

1.) Discretion

2.) Chastity

3.) Home Making

4.) Goodness

5.) Obedience

All five are tangible and yet vital in the nurturing and fortification of a marriage, as well as imparting wisdom to children a means of exemplification towards others, and service towards God.

DISCRETION

A woman who is discreet is a woman who is virtuous but also wise. Someone once said that discretion was good for the soul.

But the Bible says, "Discretion shall preserve thee," (KJV, Prov. 2:11).

In the scriptures, the word discretion is used as a synonym for the word wisdom. The Bible implies that those who know how to be discreet are wise.

I've learned over time that it's a good idea to be discreet. People shouldn't know everything about you for the simple reason most people can't handle knowing everything about you. Jesus once said to His disciples, "I have many things to say unto you, but ye cannot bear them." (KJV, John 16:12) And if Samson were here, I'm sure he would testify that telling people everything about you can lead to your downfall.

The woman who practices discretion brings honor to her husband and family by keeping the business of their household their business. It was the job of the older women to teach the younger women discretion so that they wouldn't become busybodies and gossipers. That would bring shame to the Word of God.

CHASTITY

Another lesson the older women were to teach the younger women was to live a chaste life. They were to teach them to govern their sexual behavior in a manner that would earn them the respect of their community, maintain their dignity, honor their husband, and bring glory to God.

One of the things that's missing in today's world is someone who used to be known in the African-American community as Big Momma. She was the older godly woman who not only looked after her own family but the entire community. Big Momma not only told you what to do but also what not to do.

There were things that people didn't do because they were taught by Big Momma not to do it, and they were afraid that she would find out if they did it. That kind of restraint is no longer present today in many women. And though it is a double stan-dard, society doesn't view a promiscuous woman in the same light as it does a promiscuous man.

The promiscuous man is somehow viewed in society as some-what of a much sought-after commodity. It almost seems as if he is more valuable the more promiscuous he becomes. But a woman of the same character is not elevated in value by society, but is devalued.

It's kind of like when woman buy really expensive shoes. The shoes may have cost $500 or more and at the time of purchase. In her mind, they're worth every penny she paid for them. But the more she wears them, the more wear and tear they show, the less attractive they become, and the less valuable they become to her and to everyone else.

That's the way a woman who doesn't live a chaste life is viewed by society. It doesn't matter what her initial value was; however, the more she's used the less valuable she becomes.

In contrast, the chaste woman who maintains the moral code of sexual behavior is like a fine wine. It doesn't get old, it becomes vintage; and if you've ever bought anything vintage, you know that vintage is a synonym for expensive.

What makes a bottle of wine vintage is the quality of the grapes, the skill of the winery, the length of time it's been around, and the fact that it's unopened. The fact that what's in that bottle hasn't been shared with anyone else is a primary reason why the vintage bottle of wine is so valuable to the buyer or possessor of it.

HOME MAKING

This was also a task assigned to the older women to teach the younger women. They were not only taught how to be good home-makers, but also why it was so important. These older women were to assume the role of a mother when instructing the younger women. After all, this would have been initiated in the home by the maternal parent or an older female sibling.

The basic homemaking lessons would have included instruction in cooking, sewing, cleaning, child care, gardening, and even money management. All of these areas are attested to in Proverbs 31:13-24, and it asserts that a woman of virtue is proficient in all of these areas.

But they were not only charged with teaching the how but also the why, which would serve as the motivating factor for getting the work done. The biggest reason for being a good homemaker was that it equated to good stewardship.

In the Greek, the word used is *oikonomia*. The words derived and are common to us are administrator, manager, management, house(hold), and economy. There are many examples in the Bible where God expects us to be good stewards of the things He's given to us.

One of the ways of defining stewardship is not only managing but also caring for. The virtuous woman of Proverbs 31 shows us that she's been charged with the care of three major things: a home, a husband, and children.

The woman of virtue understands that taking care of her home helps her in the care of her husband and children. Therefore, she keeps a neat and tidy home, to show both God and her husband she appreciates what's been placed in her care, even if it's not the home she desires.

She prepares good, wholesome meals for her family that are made with all the love she possesses for them, and she sees to it that she and her family is well dressed in the best she can afford. She doesn't give others an opportunity to question her love for her family, her husband's love for her and the children, or God's love for her family.

More so, being a good homemaker brings a sense of pride to her, honor to her husband, and expresses love to her children that cannot be expressed by words or money.

GOODNESS

This lesson has to do with attitude, and sad to say, this is an area where many women fail in relationships with men and where many of us fail in our dealings with other people. My mother once told me that her mother would always say, "The humble child will always taste the grace."

I didn't really know what that meant for many years, but I later learned through life and experience that grandma was saying attitude is everything. We've got to take a page from the life of the Proverbs 31 woman whose attitude was supportive, encouraging, and pleasant.

> "She will do him good and not evil all the days of her life."
> (KJV, Prov. 31:12)

The King James Bible implies that she will be good for him. In the Greek, this verse translates that "she'll be good to him." It becomes clearer when you read this verse from the Amplified Bible.

> "She comforts, encourages, and does him only good as long as there is life within her." (AMP, Prov. 31:12)

This version lets us know that we're dealing with attitude. It's not enough to have a person in your life who's discreet, chaste, and a good homemaker, but has a terrible attitude. All that other stuff is great. In fact, it's very much needed. But all of that means nothing if you have to deal with a bad attitude.

Many seemingly walk away from it all—beautiful wife, handsome husband, lovely home, great children, and a great job—but what we may not know is that they're living in their own personal hell.

The prime source of the hell maybe a bad attitude. Everybody needs someone who makes them feel special, appreciated, encouraged, and supported. For a husband, that person should be his wife. That's the basic need a husband has from his wife.

Women need security and the husband tries to provide that through providing food, money, a home, clothing, fidelity, and everything a good home needs. But men need the love of a woman who supports their dreams, goals, and ideas, as he tries to make her secure.

A man also needs a woman who knows how to talk to him. A friend of mine once told me that men want three things in a woman: "She should be saved, she should be spiritual, and she should be sweet." When you understand the nature of a man, you would have to agree with my friend's assessment of what men want in a woman.

What may not be understood is that most men are non-confrontational by nature especially with women. Men will do almost anything to avoid a confrontation with a woman. Since men hate confrontation with women, they seek a woman who possesses a sweet nature and whom they presume will never draw them into any confrontations.

In other words, he wants a woman like the one King Lemuel's mother describes to him as doing him good, and not evil.

OBEDIENCE

This is a lesson that intimidates many people, but it is a vital lesson to learn. A part of that intimidation is the simple fact that most of us don't like the idea of having to submit ourselves to anyone or anything. But I once heard my spiritual father Dr. C.E. Glover say "that blessings come on the backside of our obedience."

Personally, Dr. Glover's nugget of wisdom reinforced in me what Jesus said to His disciples:

"If ye love me, keep my commandments." (KJV, John 14:15)

I don't think Jesus said this by accident especially when you consider that in the two verses preceding verse 15. He promises to perform blessing in our lives. But notice He says these blessings will only be ours if we do two things—love Him and keep His commandments.

The word love in verse 15 can be interpreted as respect. Further more, it's possible to respect people you don't love, like a boss or even an enemy, but it's impossible to love those whom you don't respect.

That's the lesson the older women were to teach the younger women—how to love their husbands by respecting them. Many people assume that to obey or to submit means to give up your right to have an opinion or even disagree. But it simply means to respect the decision making rights of the one you've submitted to.

"Nevertheless, let everyone of you in particular so love his wife even as himself; and the wife see that she reverence her husband." KJV, Eph. 5:33

Ideally, a woman should respect the man's position as head of household to make the final decision. Yet a wife has every right to her opinion and, yes, even to disagree.

However, she shouldn't express neither her opinion or dis-agreement in the presence of others. That only emasculates the man when she does that in public—or in private, for that mat-ter. The man may react so angrily that he is incapable of receiving sound advice from her. Then it becomes a power struggle, and he will assert his natural ability to be louder and forceful in an effort to preserve his manhood.

My closing word to the readers of this book, or at least the readers of this chapter, has to do with another word from Paul's conversation with Titus on this subject of older women teaching the younger women.

The King James Bible in the fourth verse of Titus chapter 2 uses the word "sober." This word when defined is an adjective that describes our state of mind and Paul said a lot to us in this one word.

He suggests that we must not be under the influence of anything other than the Holy Spirit and common sense. Paul implies that if these lessons of love are to be carried out then we have to be in our right mind.

That is that we don't indulge so heavily in drugs or alcohol that we lose self-control of our faculties and do things that we would not ordinarily do had we been in control or in our right mind. But stress and emotions can also take control of your faculties and have you operate outside of your normal decision making process.

Therefore, if love for husband and children is to be properly expressed, and if our homes and our marriages are to be harmonious and not hellish, the virtuous woman has got to maintain her self-control, which is an added virtue.

Ten Commandments of Virtue

1. Thou shall exhibit admirable qualities.

2. Thou shall not be a gossip or a busy body.

3. Thou shall only speak wisdom to others.

4. Thou shall realize thy value.

5. Thou shall not be entangled in soul ties.

6. Thou shall be the pursued in relationships not the pursuer.

7. Thou shall not allow sex to spoil the sincere milk of a great relationship.

8. Thou shall only date men who demonstrate an ability to make a commitment.

9. Thou shall be a teacher to the young of what is good.

10. Thou shall not get bitter but better with age.

Acknowledgements

I would like to thank my wonderful and beautiful wife, Carla, who is my best friend and No. 1 fan; and my children, Remington and Zamaria, who are the joy of my life.

My parents, Mamie and the late Joseph James Sr. for their constant love and godly example and for giving my siblings and I a love for God and His church.

The outstanding church leaders who have influenced my life and ministry over the years—Larry & Evangeline Barnes, J.D. Prince, Elijah Bolden, James MacMurren, C.P. Preston and Lady Robyn Preston, Ralph W. Canty, C.E. & Lady Beaulah Glover, and Bishop Terry McCaskill.

My friend, Vernita C. Williams, who encouraged and help me start this body of work; the late Mary L. Grant, who served as my church administrator and my chief encourager.

The great staff, leaders, and congregation of Mount Hermon Missionary Baptist Church, which have given me the opportunity to grow and provide much encouragement along the way.

To my current church family at Mount Olive Missionary Baptist Church of South Miami, Florida, thank you for the warm embrace of your welcome into the city and into your hearts as your pastor.

Finally, the Lord Jesus Christ for saving me, for choosing me to be His child, and for giving me the privilege of being in His service.

INDEX

INDEX

INDEX

NOTES

NOTES

NOTES

NOTES

NOTES

NOTES

NOTES

NOTES

NOTES

NOTES

NOTES

NOTES

NOTES

NOTES

NOTES

www.ingramcontent.com/pod-product-compliance
Lightning Source LLC
Chambersburg PA
CBHW031523040426
42445CB00009B/372